Coloring Pages For Kids
Birds
Coloring Book

Coloring Books for Kids

By Gala Publication

Published by:

Gala Publication

ISBN-13: 978- 1508659426
ISBN-10: 1508659427

©Copyright 2015 – Gala Publication

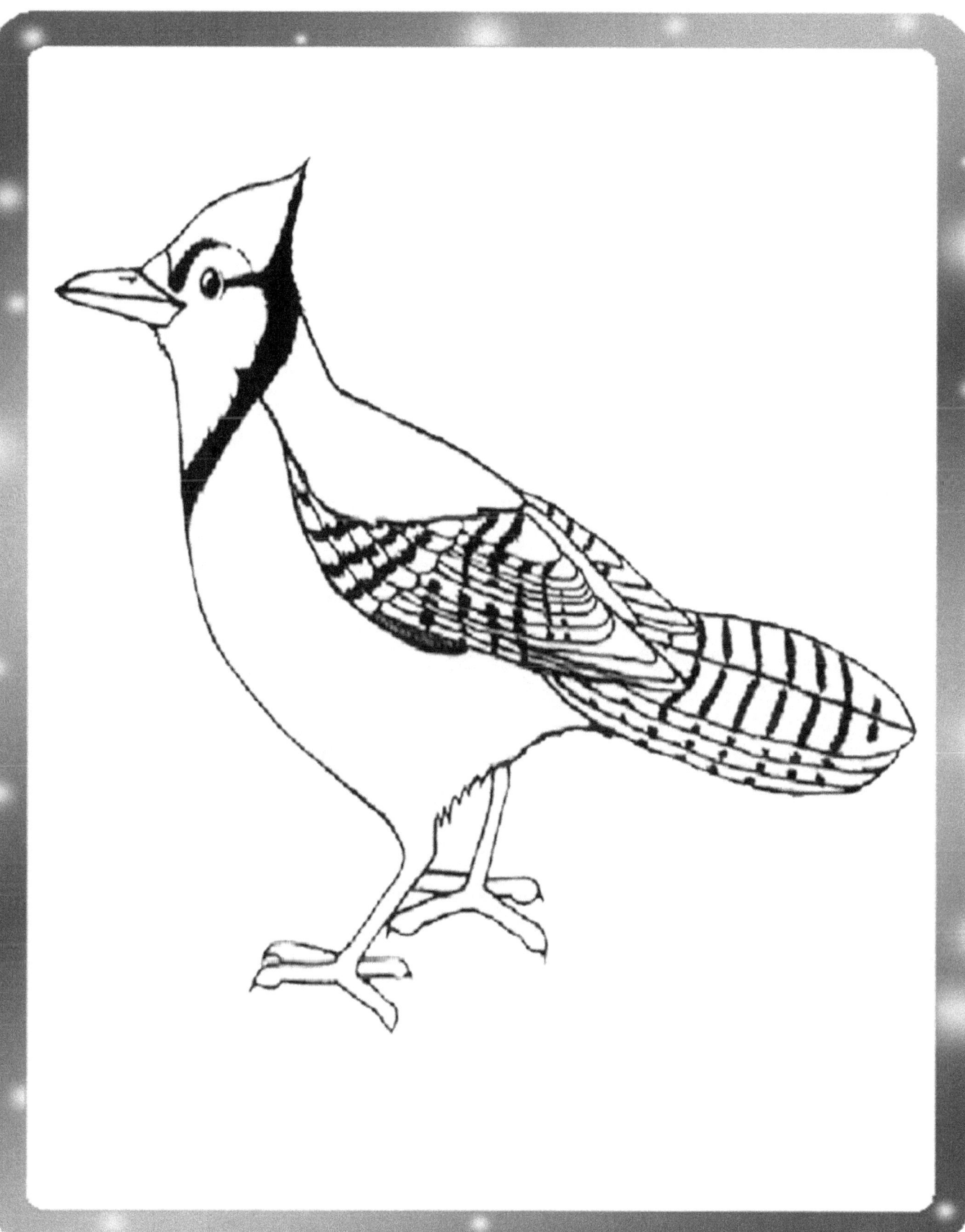

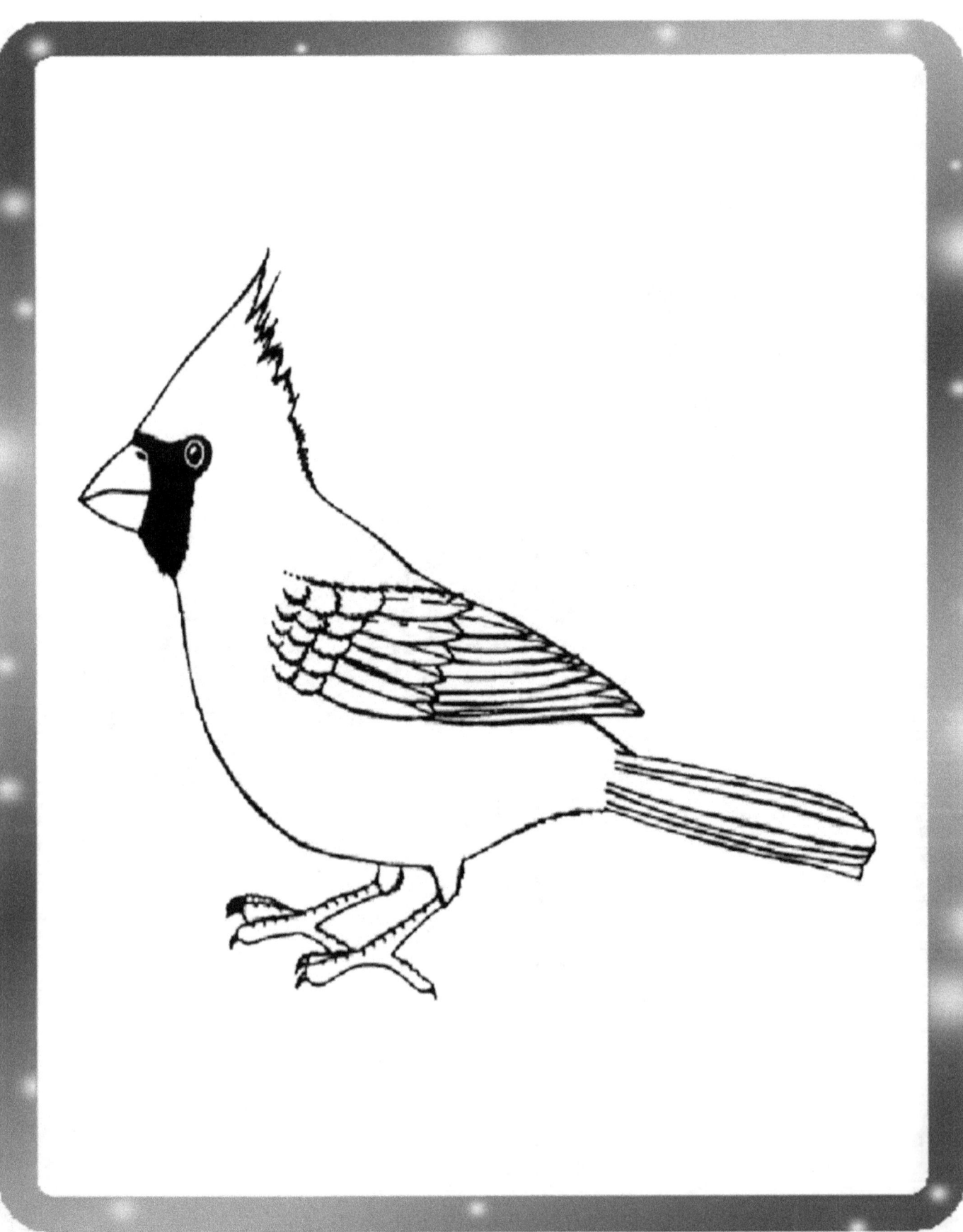

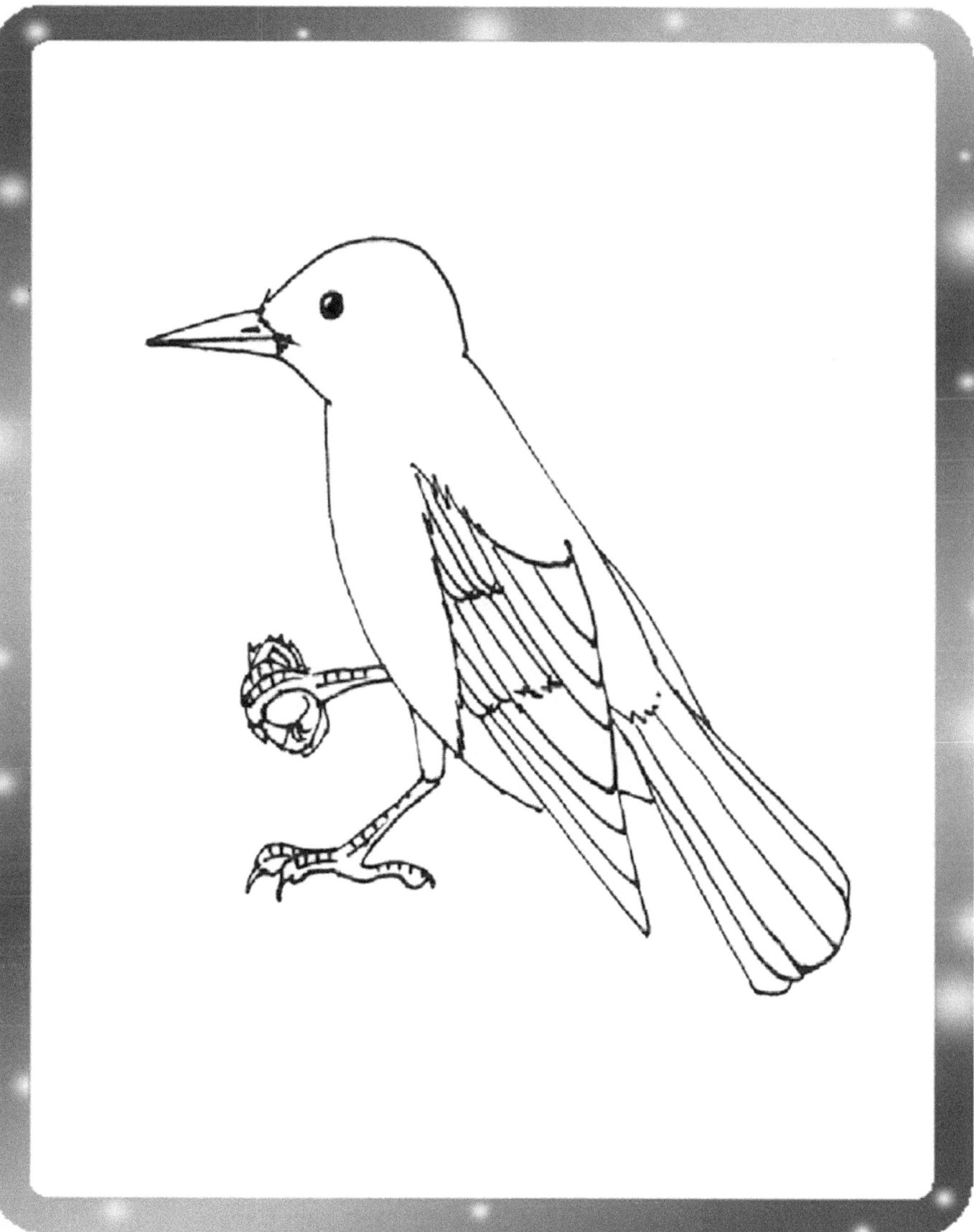

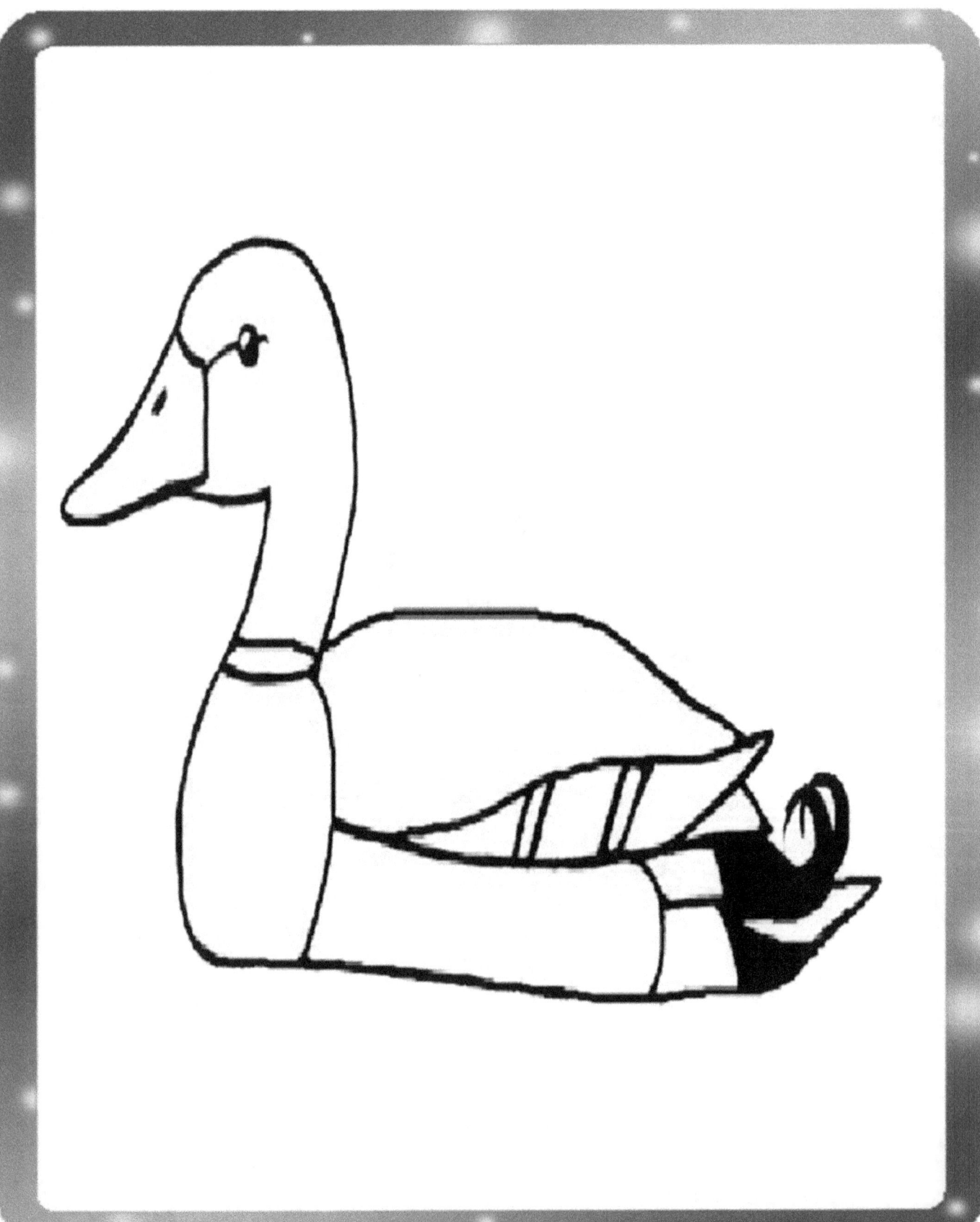

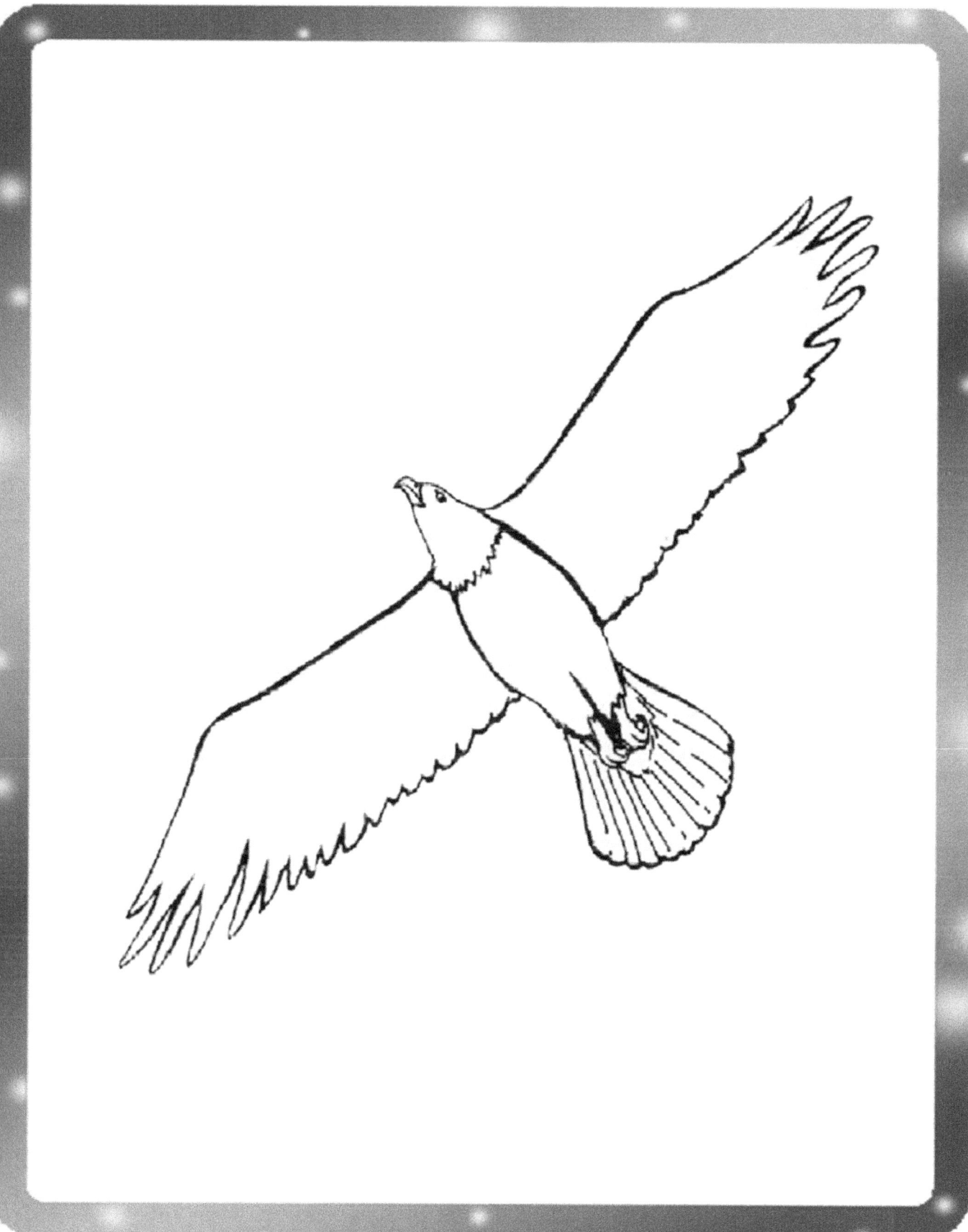

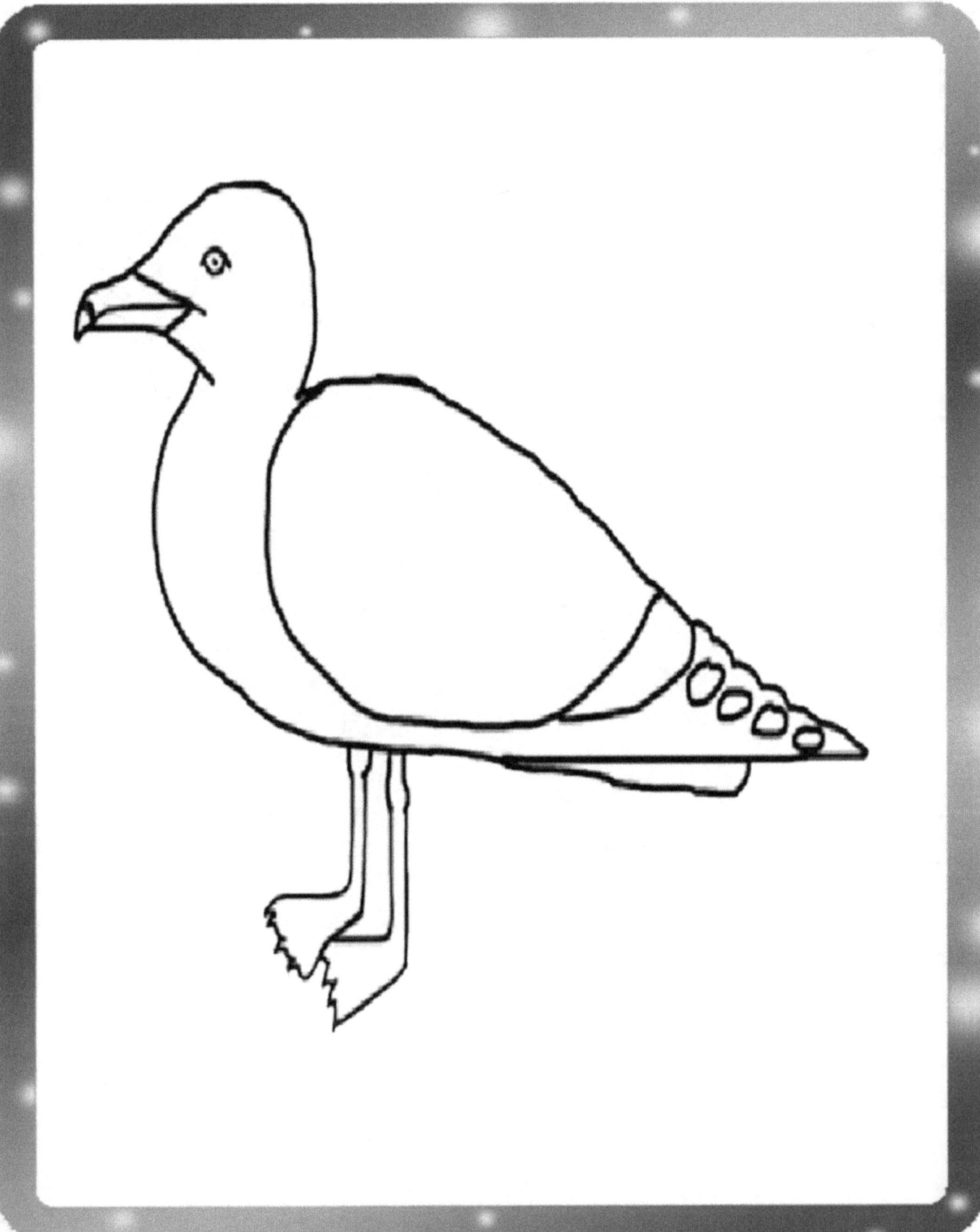

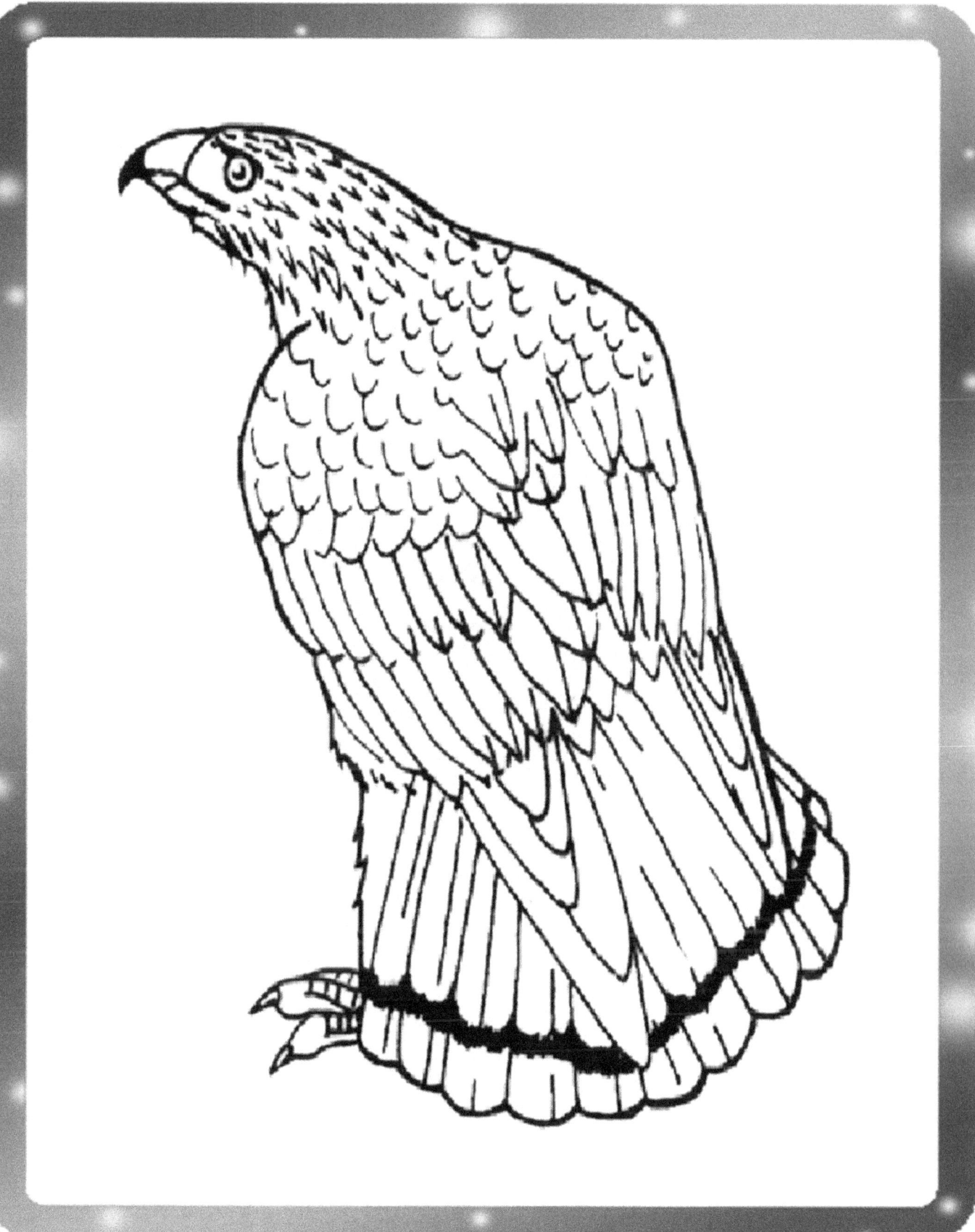

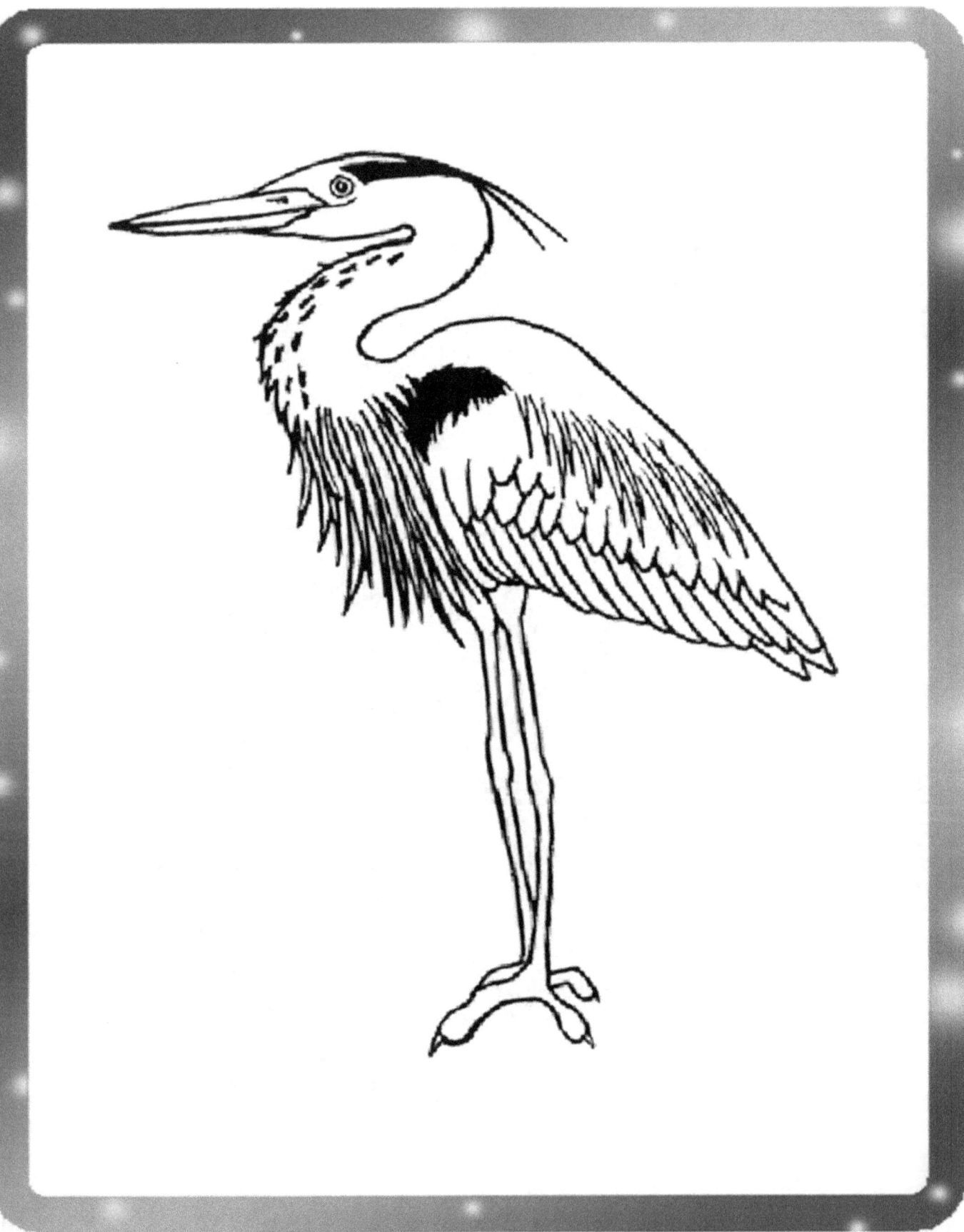

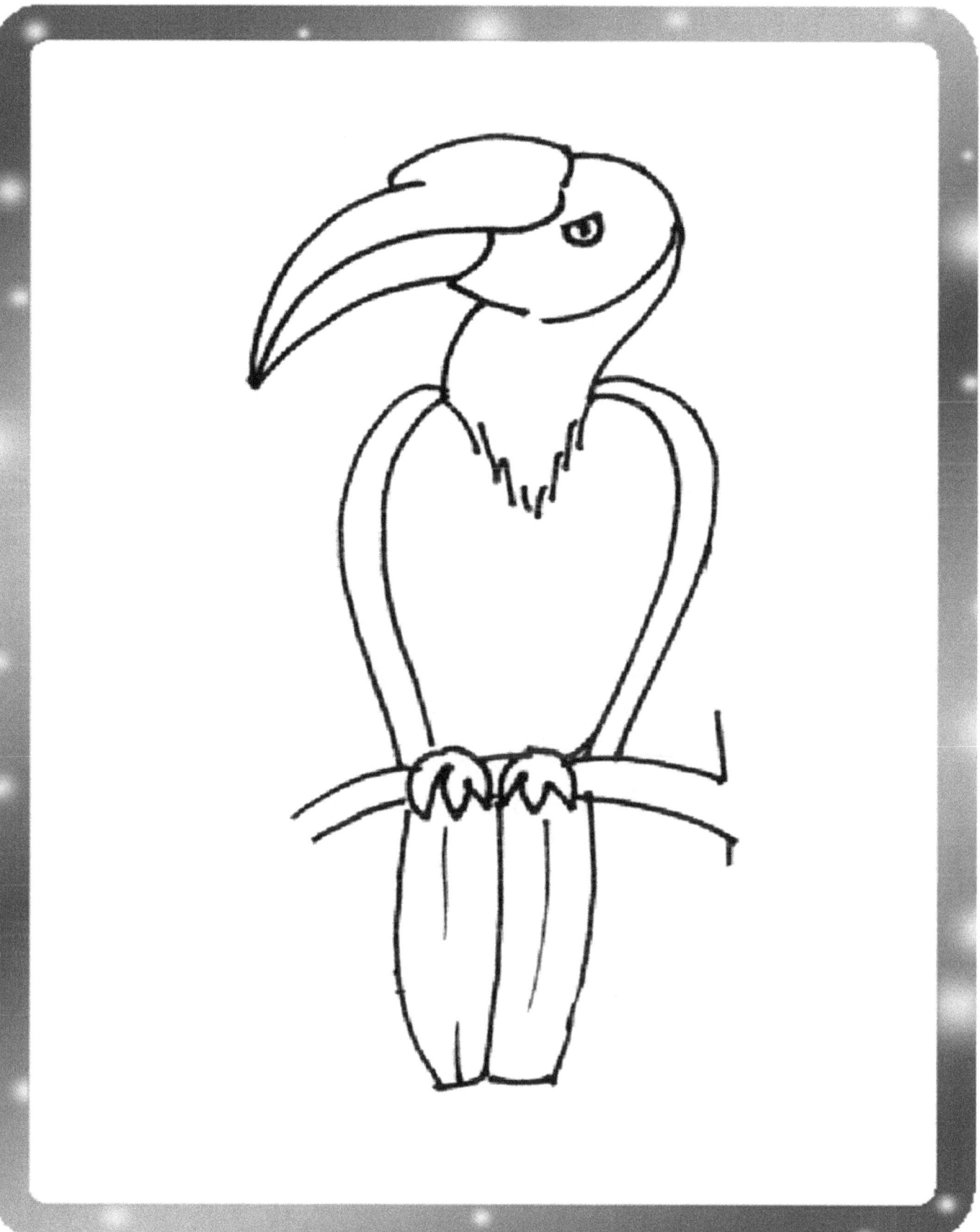

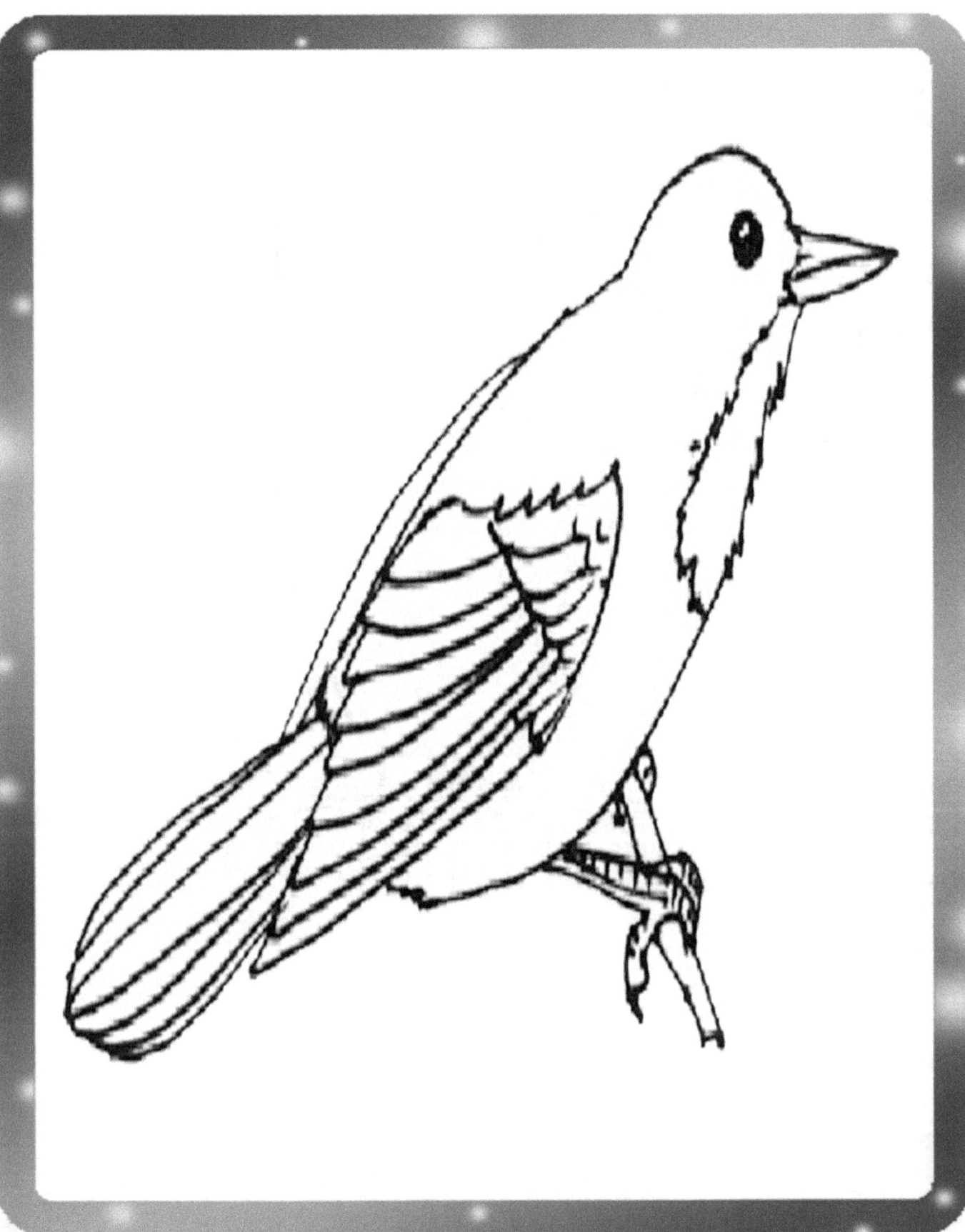

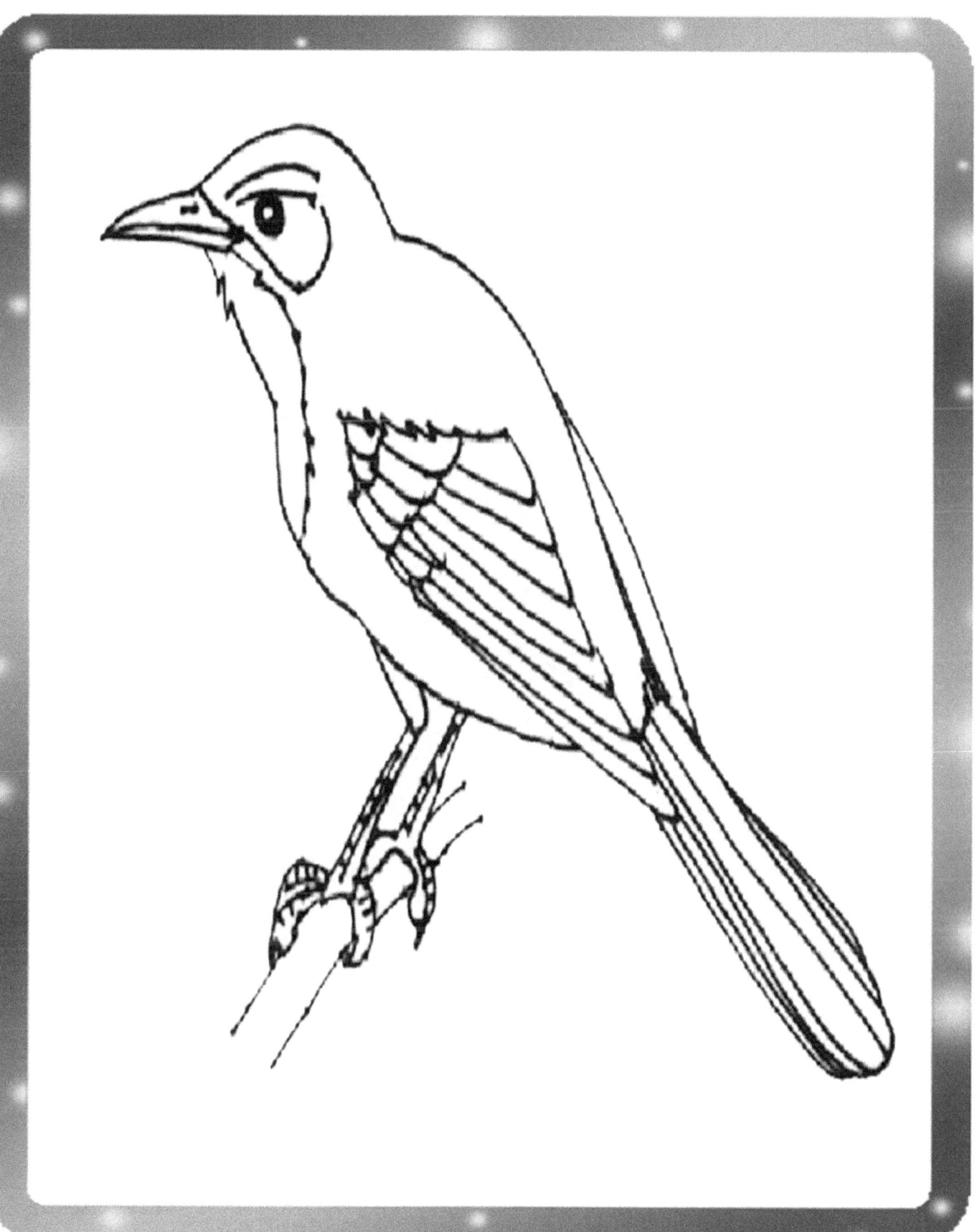

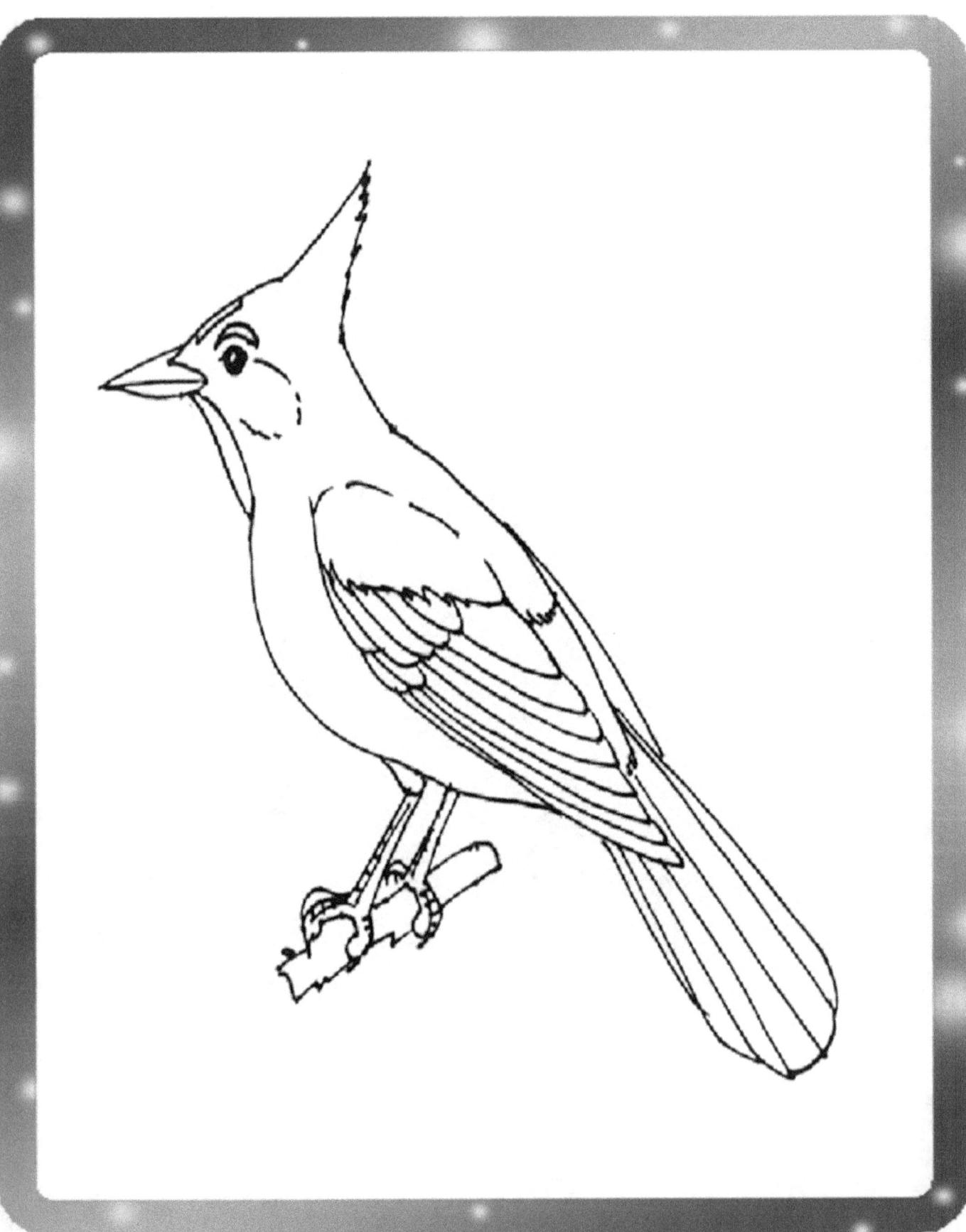

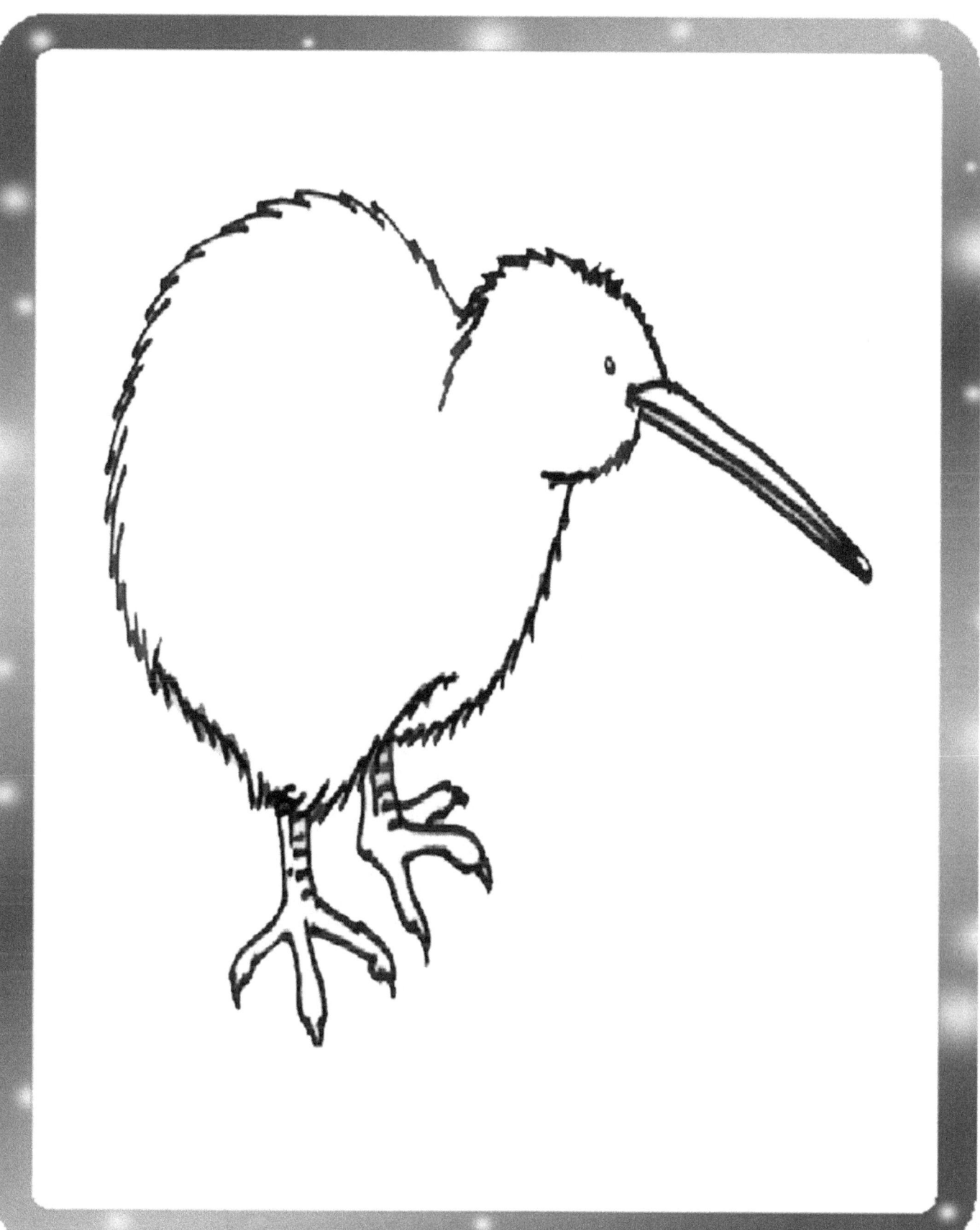

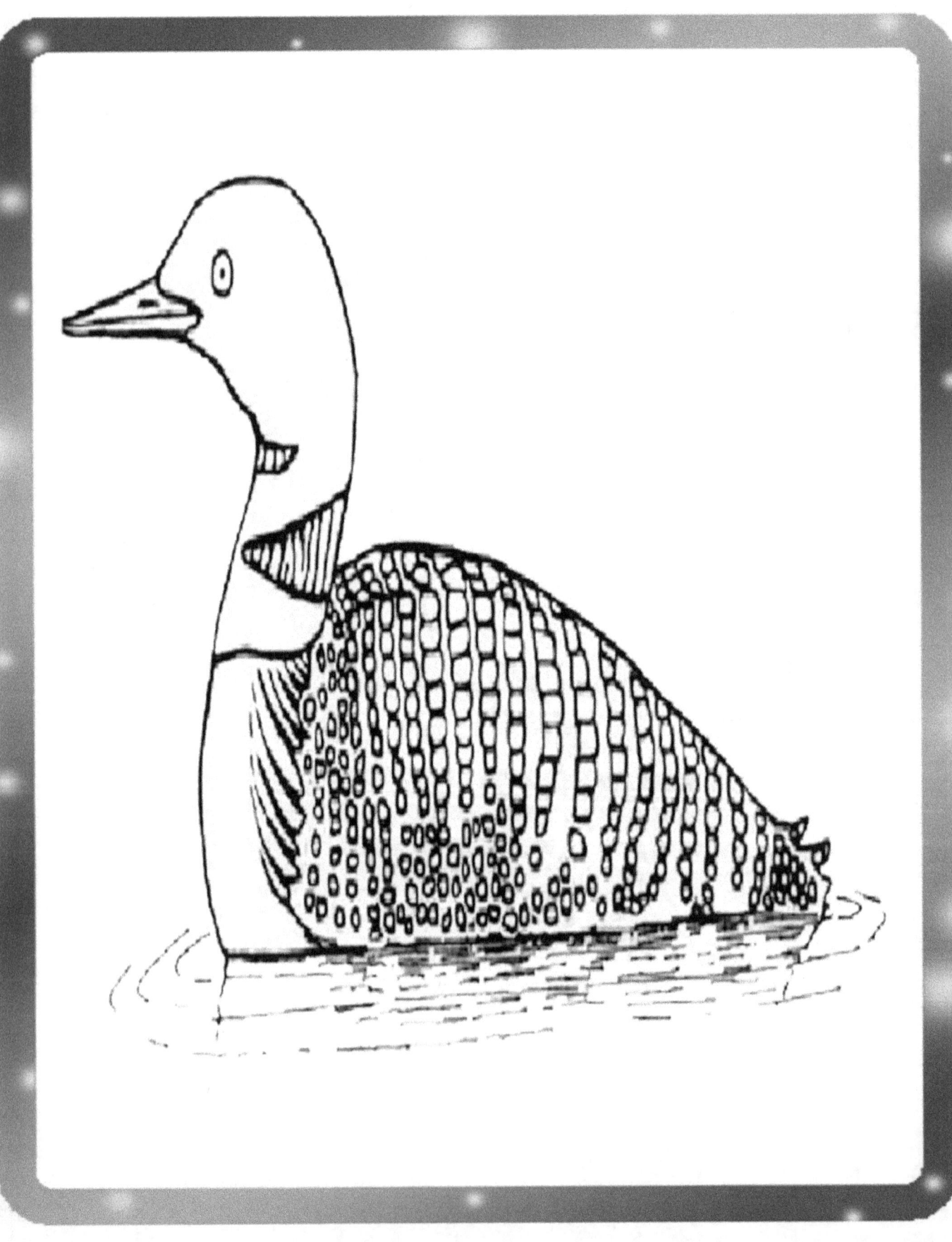

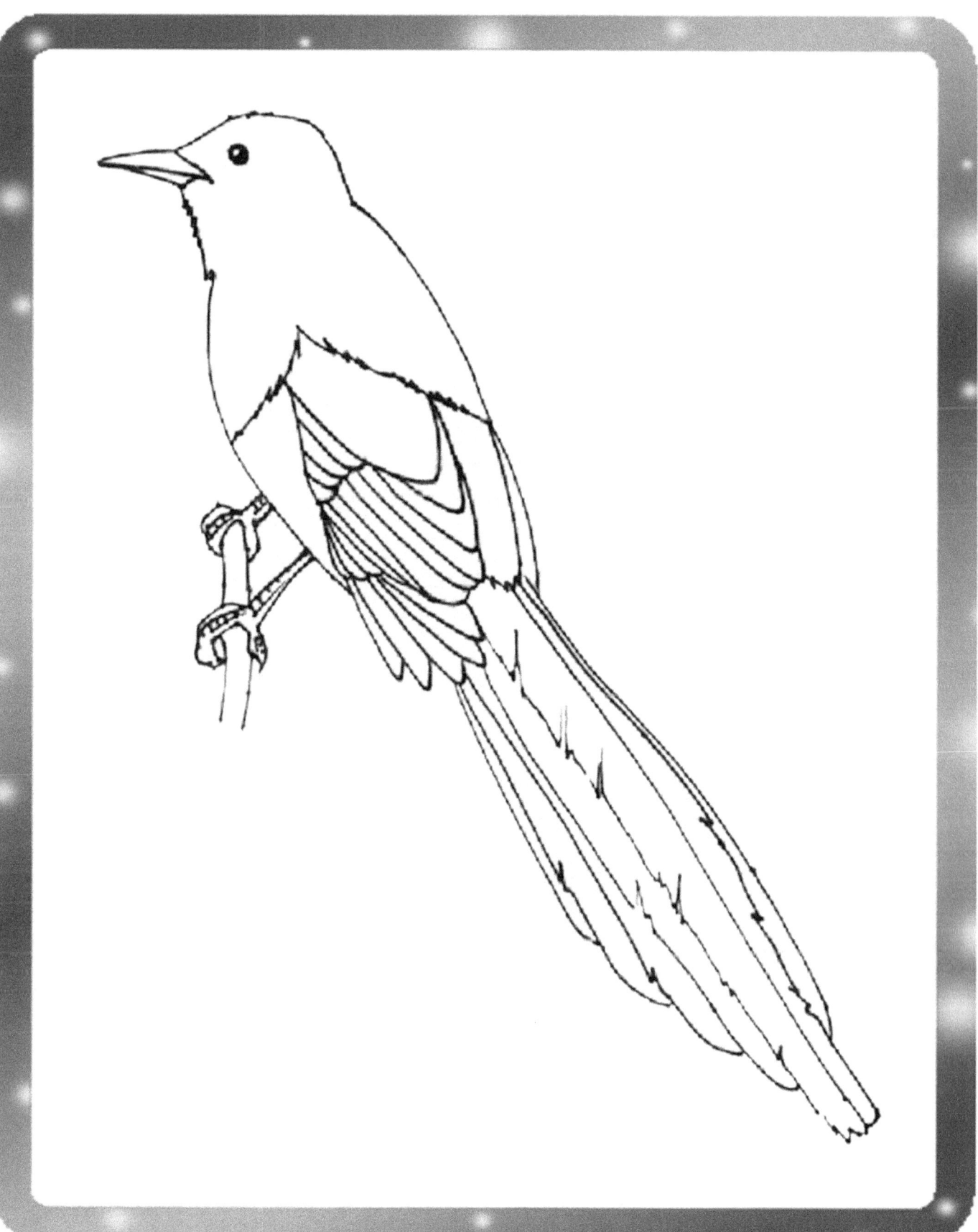

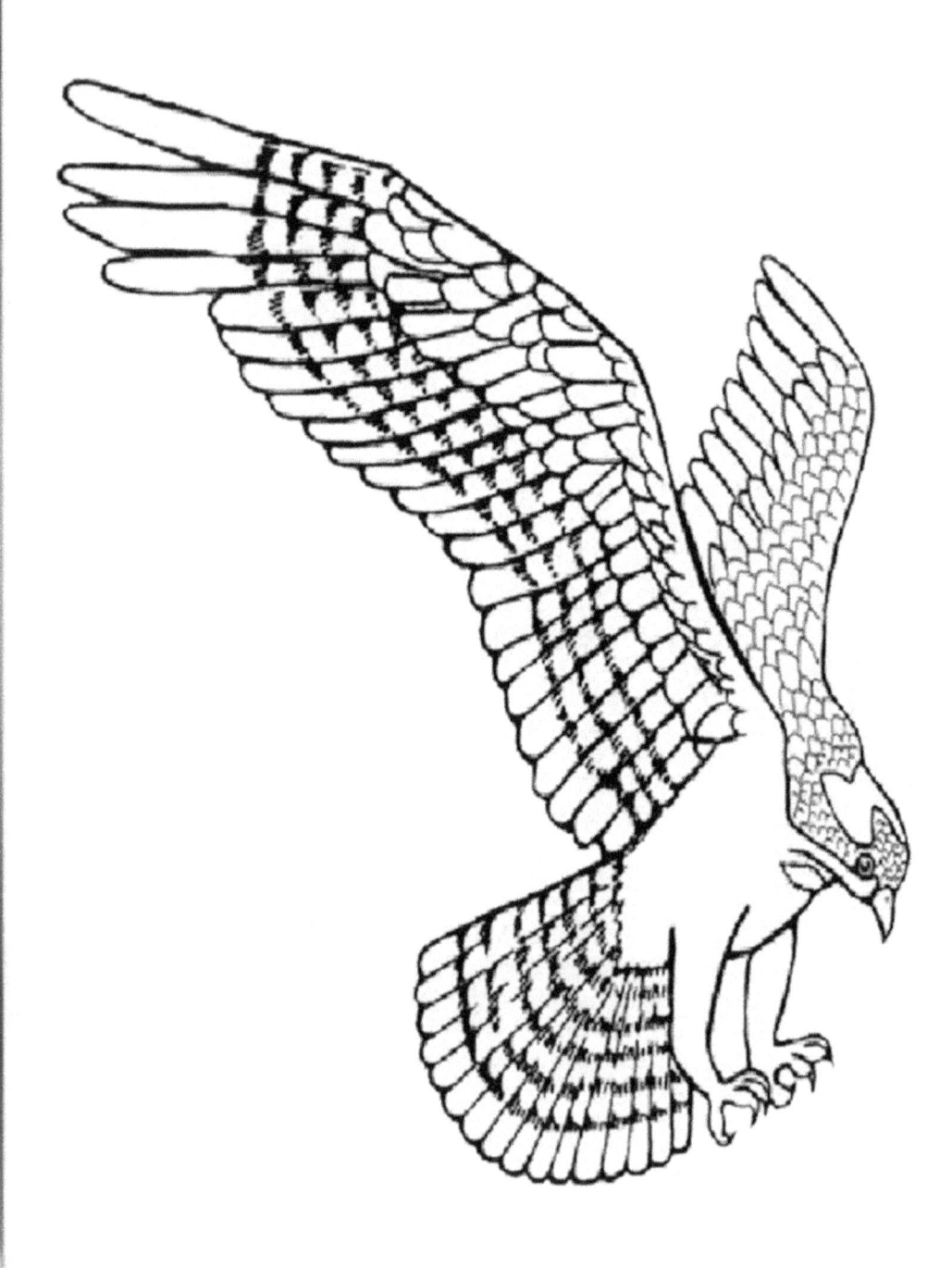

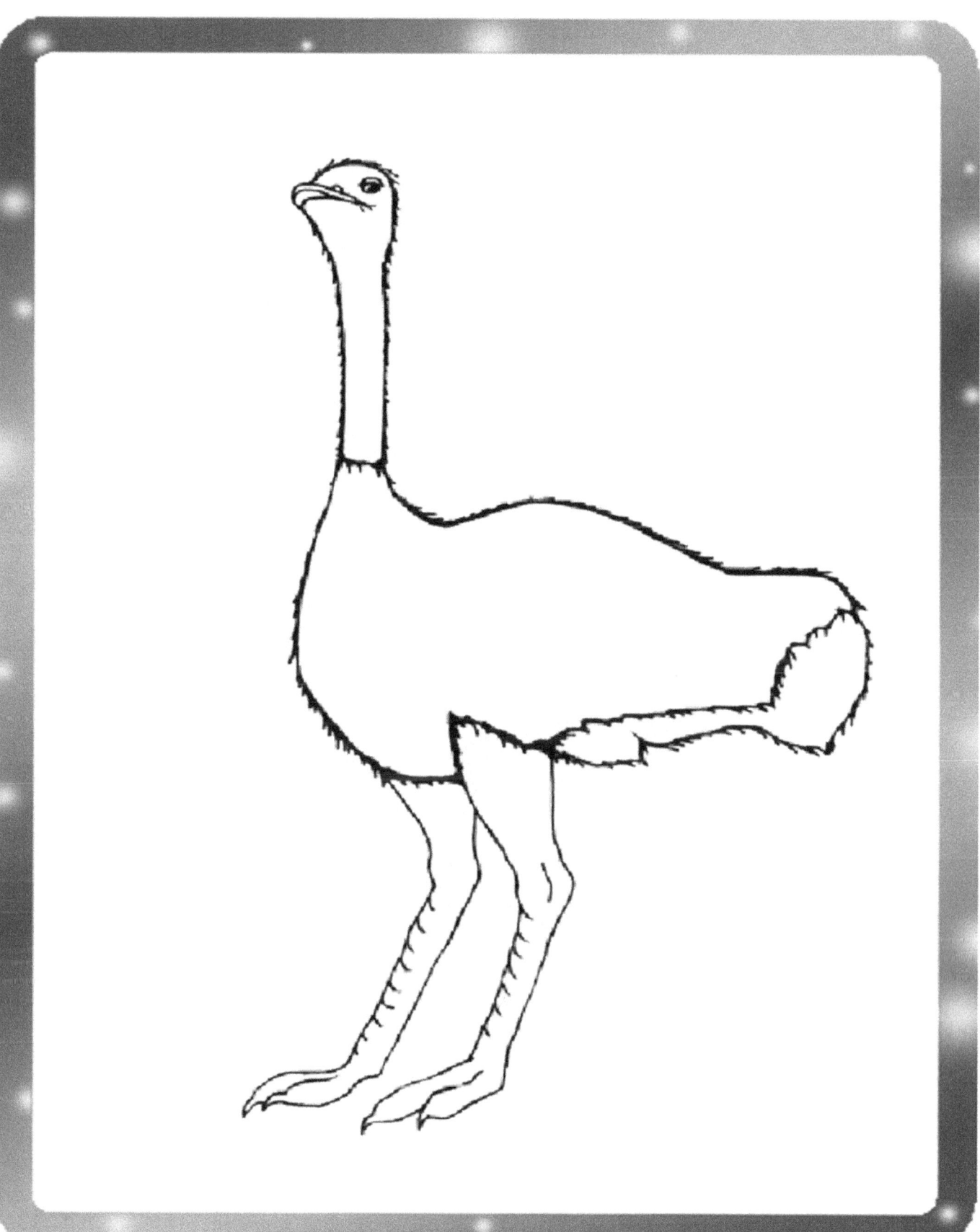

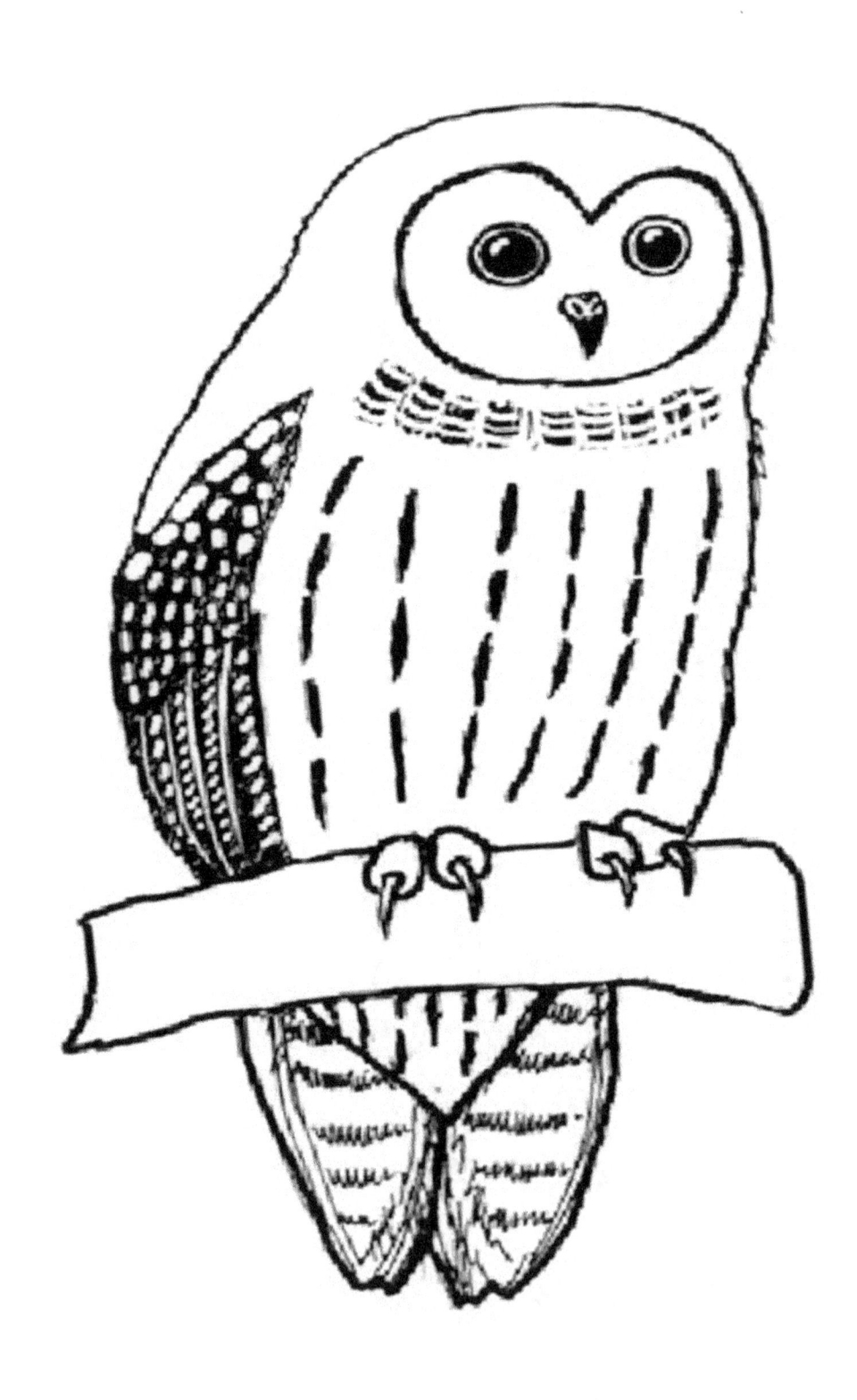

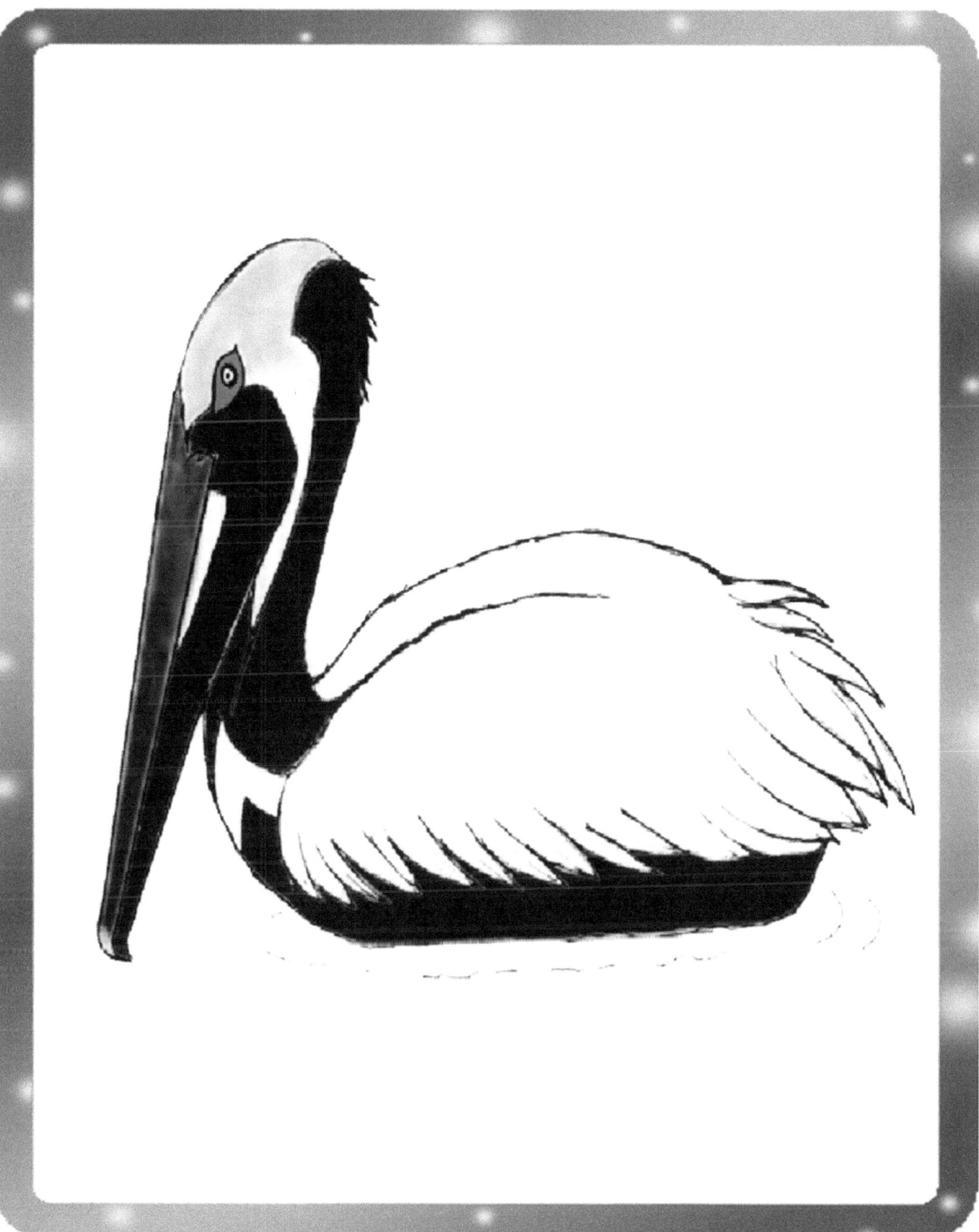

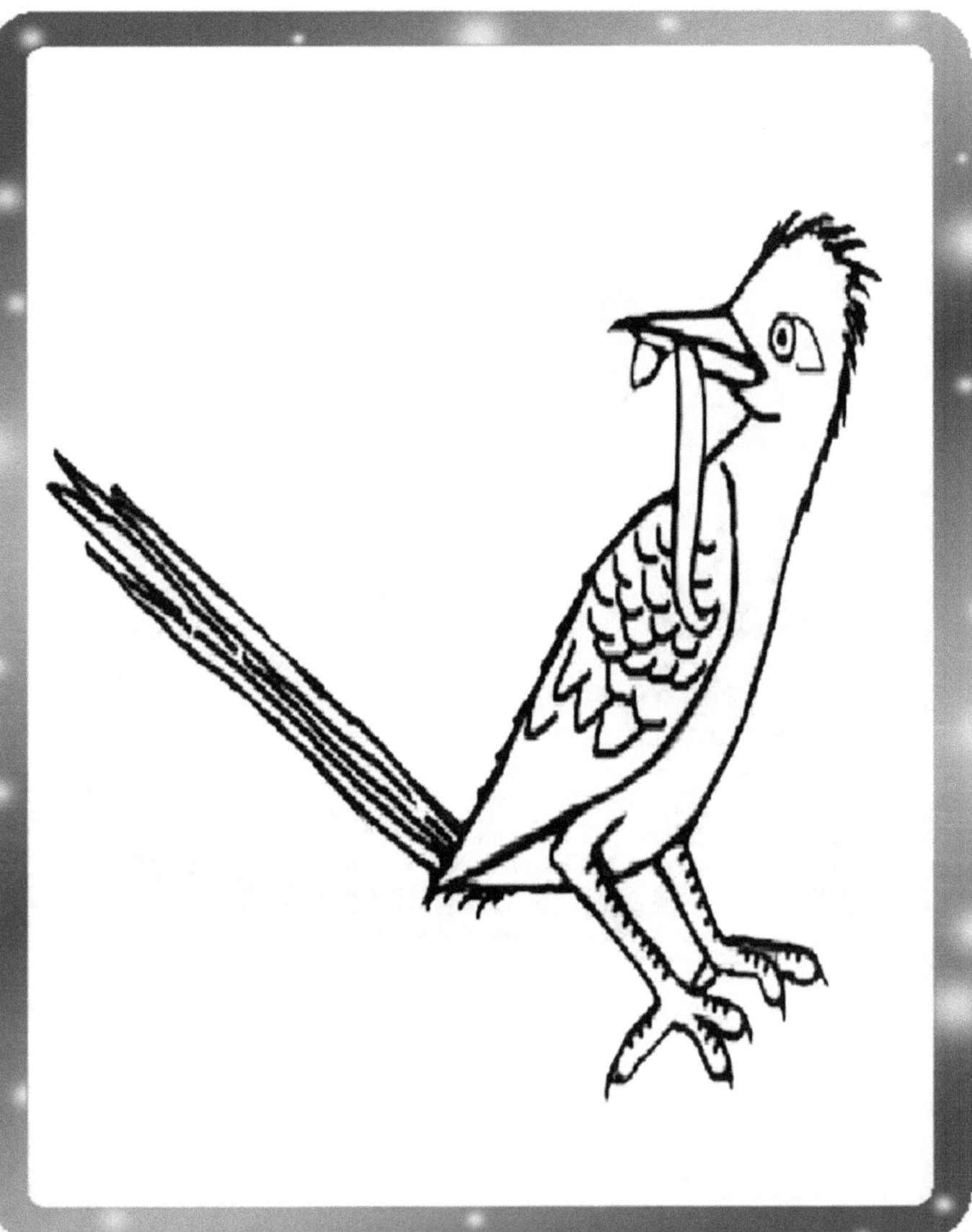

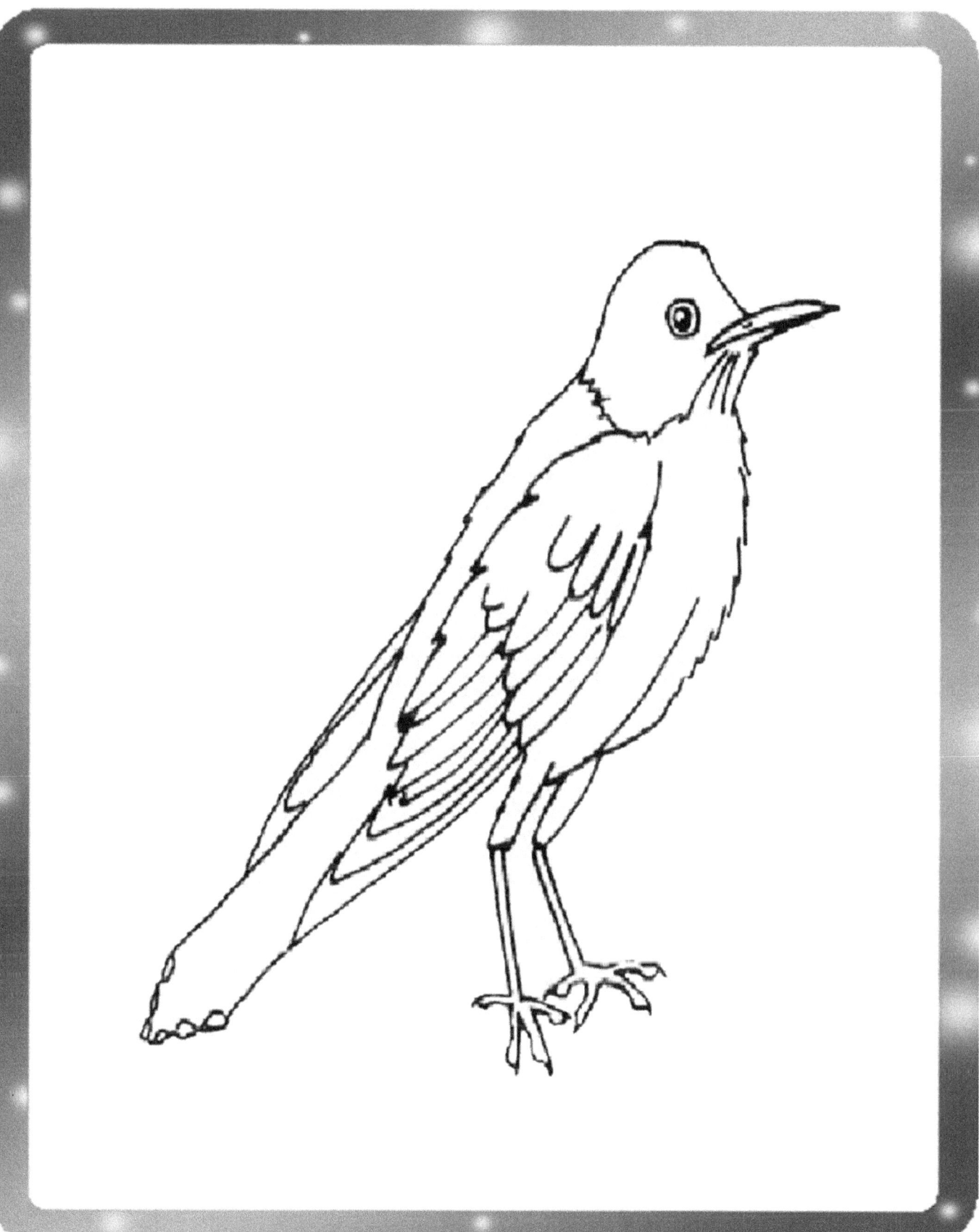

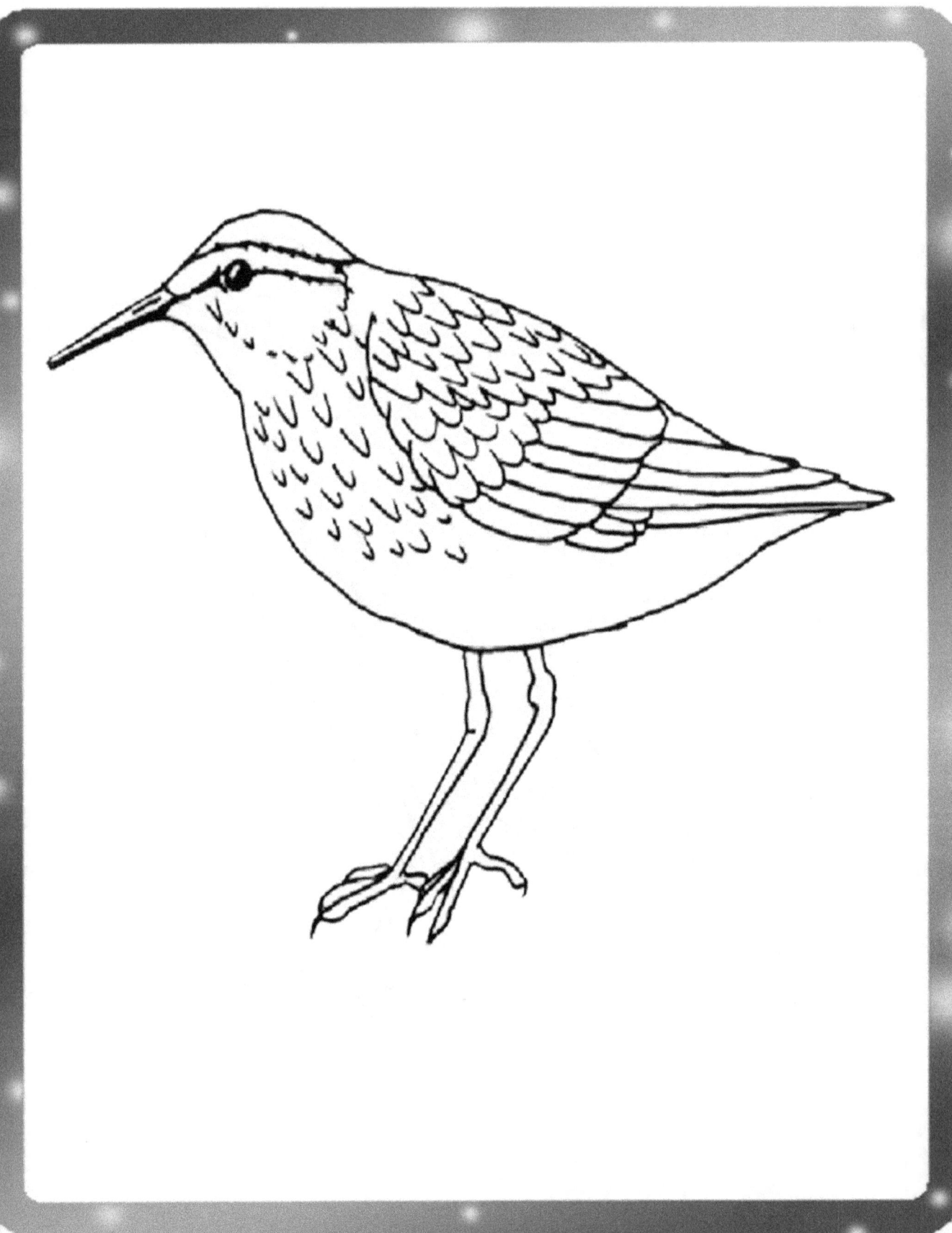

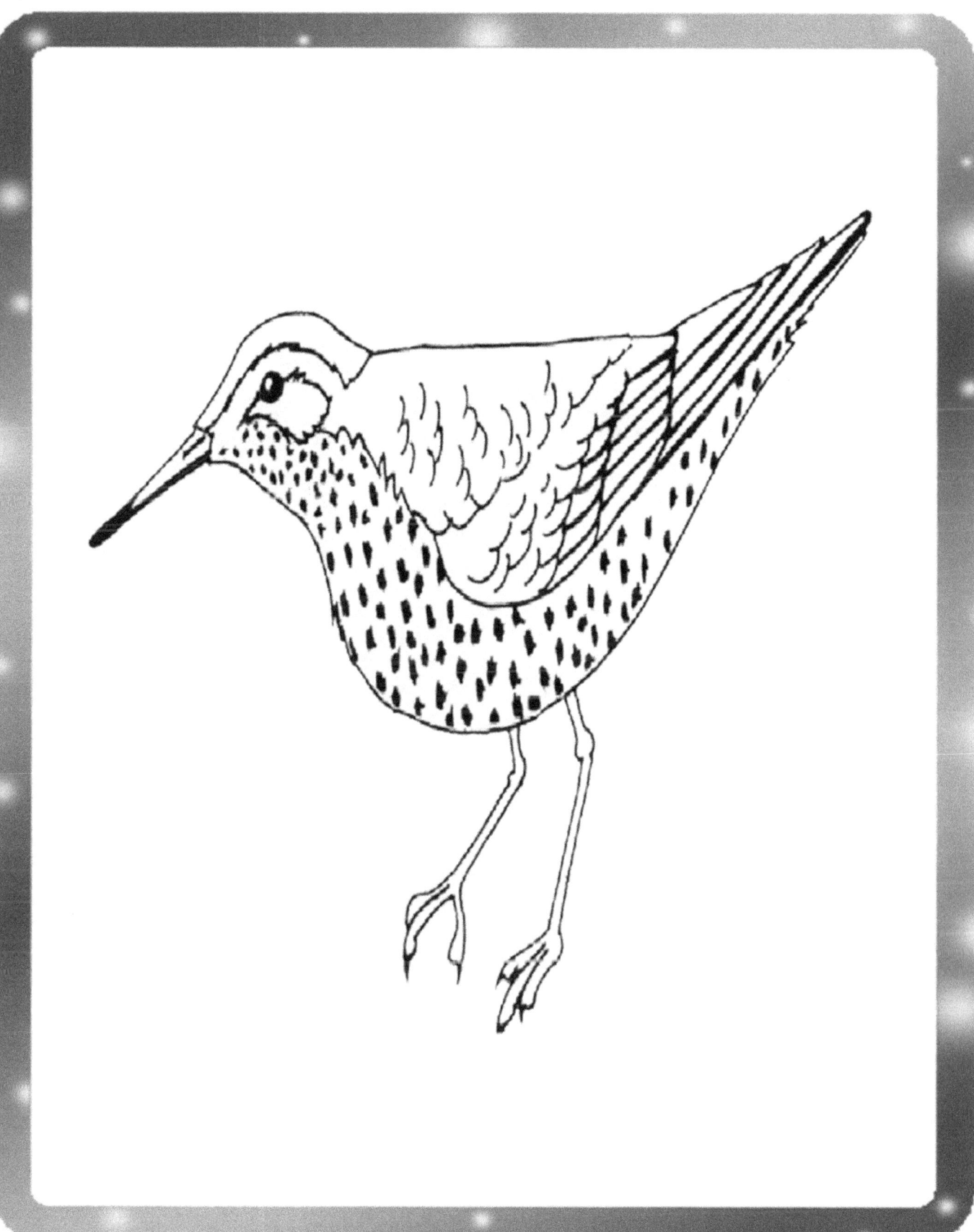

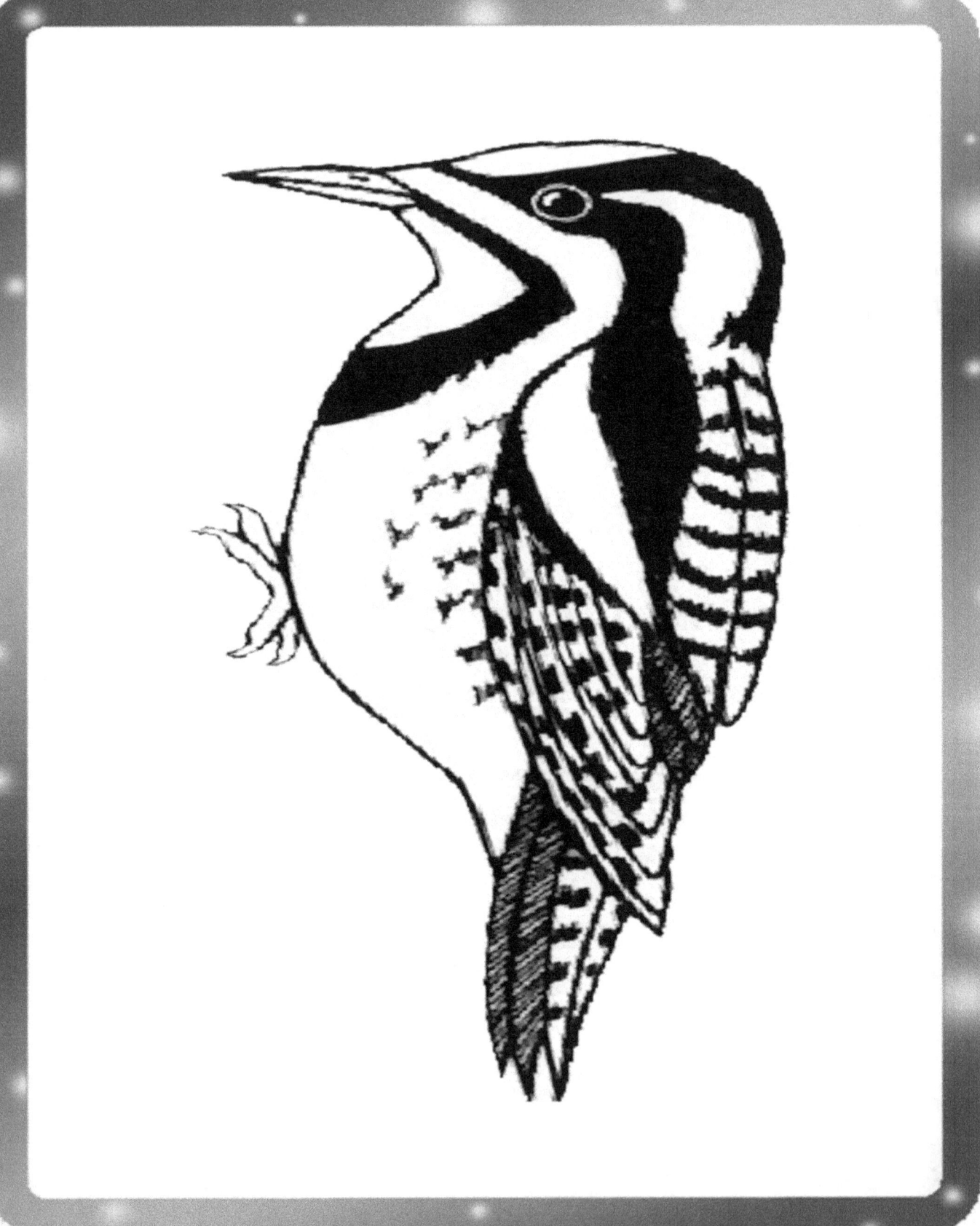

THE END

www.ingramcontent.com/pod-product-compliance
Lightning Source LLC
Chambersburg PA
CBHW080627180526
45168CB00007B/3082